BACK TO YOUR
ROOTS!

BACK TO YOUR ROOTS!

DELICIOUS ROOT VEGETABLE RECIPES

This edition published by Parragon Books Inc. in 2014 and distributed by

Parragon Inc.
440 Park Avenue South, 13th Floor
New York, NY 10016
www.parragon.com/lovefood

LOVE FOOD is an imprint of Parragon Books Ltd

ISBN 978-1-4723-2988-2

Printed in China

New recipes written by Sarah Bush
Introduction and incidental text by Christine McFadden
New photography by Mike Cooper
New home economy by Lincoln Jefferson
Additional design work by Geoff Borin
Internal and jacket flap illustrations by Julie Ingham and Nicola O'Byrne

Notes for the Reader
This book uses standard kitchen measuring spoons and cups. All spoon and cup measurements are level unless otherwise indicated. Unless otherwise stated, milk is assumed to be whole, eggs are large, individual vegetables are medium, and pepper is freshly ground black pepper. Unless otherwise stated, all root vegetables should be peeled prior to using.

Garnishes, decorations, and serving suggestions are all optional and not necessarily included in the recipe ingredients or method. The times given are only an approximate guide. Preparation times differ according to the techniques used by different people and the cooking times may also vary from those given. Optional ingredients, variations, or serving suggestions have not been included in the time calculations.

Picture acknowledgments
The publisher would like to thank the following for the permission to reproduce copyright material: Front and back cover illustrations courtesy of iStock; page 13: Different vegetables in a crate © Beyond fotomedia/Junos; page 75: Still life of carrots and beets in a colander © Aurora Open/Justin Baille; page 112: Organic assorted beets © The Agency Collection/Mint Images/Tim Pannell; page 113: Radishes © Image Source.

CONTENTS

Introduction   6

The Ultimate in Comfort   10

Home From Work & Hungry   40

Let Me Entertain You   68

On the Side   98

Index   128

LET'S GET TO THE ROOT OF THE MATTER!

We tend to think of root vegetables as homey comfort foods, but these buried treasures have surprisingly feisty flavors and come in an artist's palette of colors. Botanically speaking, they are not all roots. Some are tubers—the swollen tips of underground stems. These include potatoes, yams, and Jerusalem artichokes, whereas beets, carrots, and radishes are straightforward roots.

BEET

Beet comes in familiar garnet red, plus golden yellow, white, and stunning pink-and-white candy stripes. Its slightly odd flavor is sweet and earthy, with a little background bitterness. It goes well with horseradish, buttermilk, juniper, and dill.

CARROT

Not only do carrots help you see in the dark, they come in an assortment of shapes, sizes, and colors and not just regulation orange. There are yellow, red, purple, and white varieties, too. Raw or cooked, they look stunning on the plate.

CELERIAC

With its pock-marked skin and hairy tangle of roots, celeriac (sometimes called celery root) is not the most beautiful of vegetables, but the flavor more than makes up for its looks. It's the root to go for when you want the freshness of celery along with the starchy comfort of potato.

JERUSALEM ARTICHOKE

These elongated tubers are an undistinguished beige, although some are a more striking reddish pink. They have a unique, earthy, nutty flavor, similar to globe artichokes.

PARSNIP

A quietly understated vegetable, parsnips may be slim and tapering, or wide-shoulder heavyweights. The ivory flesh has a clean taste that is sweet without being cloying.

POTATO

Potatoes range from monster bakers to pebble-size new potatoes. The skin may be familiar beige, rosy pink, or red, or sometimes blue or purple, with ivory, buttery yellow, or even purple flesh. Textures also vary. Some are mealy, such as russets, and perfect for mashing, others are creamy, such as Yukon gold, suited for soups; waxy new potatoes are ideal for salads.

RADISH

Radishes span a spectrum of sizes, shapes, and colors. There are small, mild red-skinned varieties, large black-skinned Asian ones, and exotic types with green or red flesh. They all have a crisp juicy texture with a peppery flavor that varies in intensity.

RUTABAGA

Recognizable by the two-tone skin—purple on top and a dusky yellow below—the rutabaga is an underused root with dense golden flesh and a peppery flavor. It is delicious mashed, roasted, or fried, or even grated raw in salads.

SWEET POTATO

The most common of these torpedo-shape tubers have thick, brownish orange skin with vivid orange, moist, sweet flesh. They are good roasted, mashed, or baked, and also work well in sweet dishes, especially pies.

TURNIP

Related to the rutabaga and radish, turnips vary in shape—some are flat like spinning tops, others are round or elongated. The flesh is less dense than rutabaga with a sweeter, mellower flavor.

YAM

The yam is a versatile tropical tuber with a rough brown skin and sticky, creamy white flesh. It can be boiled, baked, fried, or mashed just like normal potatoes.

7

FEEL THE BENEFIT

There's no question about the strong link between good health and a diet rich in vegetables. Together with fruit, vegetables feature in the nutritional guidelines of all major countries, and experts universally agree that eating more of them may help protect against chronic and life-threatening diseases, such as heart disease and cancer.

Vegetables not only provide vitamins, minerals, and fiber, they also contain antioxidants, a nutrient group that protects the body by deactivating substances known as free radicals. It's believed that they attack DNA, the genetic material in the nucleus of a cell, and the resulting changes may cause cancer. Free radicals also cause oxidative damage linked to premature aging, cataracts, and hardening of the arteries.

Although often overlooked, root vegetables have excellent nutritional credentials. They all contain slow-release carbohydrates that make you feel full and keep your energy levels stable. Most have a desirably low glycemic index score, with the exceptions being potatoes and parsnips. You can substitute sweet potato for these if you are tracking your GI score.

Roots are packed with health-promoting fiber, both the cholesterol-lowering soluble kind, and the insoluble type that used to be called "roughage"— the most helpful for dealing with constipation. Superfibrous types—old carrots and parsnips, for example—also contain a woody

substance called lignin, found in the core. It's thought to lower blood cholesterol levels and, therefore, the risk of clogged-up arteries.

Some root vegetables have special properties. Beets, for example, contains a group of color pigments known as betalains. These have antioxidant and anti-inflammatory properties, but also trigger enzymes that bind together harmful substances in the cells and make them more easily excreted from the body.

As the name suggests, carrots are rich in carotenoids, as are orange-flesh sweet potatoes. Carotenoids include not just the better-known beta-carotene, which is converted to vitamin A in the body, but alpha-carotene and lutein, too, valued for their cancer-fighting properties. A daily carrot is also believed to improve night vision.

THE ULTIMATE IN COMFORT

Veg Out! 12

Celeriac Soup with Cheese Pastry Sticks 14

Sweet Potato & Apple Soup 16

Jerusalem Artichoke Soup 18

Roasted Root Soup with Ginger 20

Beet Borscht Soup 22

Potato & Corn Fritters with Relish 24

Carrot Sausages & Mashed Potatoes 26

Sweet Potato Pancakes 28

Get Fresh! 30

Yam & Beef Stew with Couscous 32

Beet Burgers in a Bun 34

Jerusalem Artichokes with Tomato Sauce 36

Yam-Topped Beef Casserole 38

VEG OUT!

Root vegetables are relatively inexpensive and have a reasonable shelf life, so there are plenty of places to buy them.

IN THE CITY

Large supermarkets are an obvious choice, but there are other options. Shops selling African or Asian vegetables are a treasure trove. You'll find yams, with a host of root vegetables that you may never have set eyes on before. They are all worth a try. Even the largest cities will usually have a farmers' market, filled with fresh vegetables. Keep in mind that root vegetables do not do well in an overheated, brightly lit environment, so avoid those sold in the typical local convenience store.

IN THE COUNTRY

For freshness and seasonality, it's hard to beat a good farm shop. The vegetables will probably have been grown on the farm, or within a defined radius. Buying direct from the farm also reduces food miles, although this is a double-edged sword if you think of the miles involved getting to and from the farm. There is certainly less waste. Farmers sell vegetables regardless of cosmetic irregularities, and without unnecessary packaging to dispose of when you get home.

IN A BOX

If you have little time, an alternative is arranging for home delivery of vegetable boxes. Subscribers regularly receive a box containing whatever vegetables are in season. You can usually choose the size of box to suit your lifestyle, or veto a vegetable if you don't like it. Invariably you will need to use your imagination to come up with different ways of cooking the same vegetable, particularly if it has a long season.

BUYING ORGANIC

Root vegetables absorb herbicides, pesticides, and fungicides that end up in the soil, so you may want to consider buying organic ones, especially if you eat a particular type every day. They are more expensive but generally come out with flying colors in taste trials. You'll find organic vegetables in good supermarkets, but they are likely to have clocked up food miles. You may do better to try a good health food store or an organic farm or farmers' market if there is one near you.

CELERIAC SOUP WITH CHEESE PASTRY STICKS

SERVES: 4　　　　**PREP TIME: 15 MINS**　　　　**COOK TIME: 45 MINS**

INGREDIENTS

3 tablespoons olive oil

1 onion, chopped

1 celeriac, cut into chunks

4 cups vegetable stock

1 small bunch fresh thyme, chopped

salt and pepper, to taste

fresh thyme sprigs, to garnish

CHEESE STICKS

1 pound ready-to-bake puff pastry, thawed if frozen

all-purpose flour, for dusting

1 egg, beaten

1 cup finely grated Parmesan cheese

butter, for greasing

pepper

1. Heat the oil in a large saucepan over medium heat, add the onion, and sauté, stirring frequently, for 4–5 minutes, until soft but not browned.

2. Add the celeriac and sauté, stirring frequently, for 3–4 minutes. Pour in the stock and add the thyme. Simmer for 25 minutes, or until the celeriac is tender. Meanwhile, preheat the oven to 400°F.

3. To make the cheese sticks, thinly roll out the pastry on a floured work surface. Brush with half the egg, sprinkle with half the cheese, and season well with pepper.

4. Fold the pastry in half. Brush with the remaining egg, sprinkle with the remaining cheese, and season with pepper. Lightly grease and line two baking sheets.

5. Cut the pastry into strips about ½-inch wide. Twist gently along their length to produce spirals. Place on the prepared baking sheets and bake in the preheated oven for 5 minutes, or until crisp and golden.

6. Puree the soup in the pan using a handheld blender and gently reheat. Season with salt and pepper. Ladle the soup into warm bowls, garnish with thyme sprigs, and serve with the warm pastry sticks.

SWEET POTATO & APPLE SOUP

SERVES: 6   **PREP TIME: 15 MINS**   **COOK TIME: 45 MINS**

INGREDIENTS

1 tablespoon butter

3 leeks, thinly sliced

1 large carrot, thinly sliced

4 sweet potatoes, diced

2 Granny Smith apples, peeled, cored, and diced

5 cups water

freshly grated nutmeg, to taste

1 cup apple juice

1 cup light cream

salt and pepper, to taste

snipped fresh chives or cilantro, to garnish

1. Melt the butter in a large saucepan over medium–low heat.

2. Add the leeks, cover, and cook for 6–8 minutes, or until soft, stirring frequently.

3. Add the carrot, sweet potatoes, apples, and water. Lightly season with salt, pepper, and nutmeg. Bring to a boil, reduce the heat, and simmer, covered, for about 20 minutes, stirring occasionally, until the vegetables are tender.

4. Let the soup cool slightly, then puree in the pan with a handheld blender.

5. Stir in the apple juice, place over low heat, and simmer for about 10 minutes, until heated through.

6. Stir in the cream and simmer for an additional 5 minutes, stirring frequently, until heated through. Taste and adjust the seasoning, if necessary.

7. Ladle the soup into warm bowls, garnish with chives, and serve.

HERO TIPS

This soup is great for using up any excess apples you may have after a good apple season. You can also garnish the soup with thin, sweet apple slices.

JERUSALEM ARTICHOKE SOUP

SERVES: 4-6   **PREP TIME: 15 MINS**   **COOK TIME: 45 MINS**

INGREDIENTS

4 tablespoons butter

2 onions, chopped

4½ cups sliced Jerusalem artichokes, dropped into water to prevent discoloration

3½ cups vegetable stock

1¼ cups milk

salt and pepper, to taste

CROUTONS

¼ cup vegetable oil

2 slices of day-old white bread, crusts removed, bread cut into ½-inch cubes

1. To make the croutons, heat the oil in a skillet over medium heat. Add the bread cubes in a single layer and sauté, tossing occasionally, until golden brown and crisp.

2. Remove the pan from the heat and transfer the croutons onto paper towels to drain.

3. Melt the butter in a large saucepan over medium heat. Add the onions and cook until soft.

4. Add the drained artichokes and mix well with the butter. Cover the pan and cook slowly over low heat for about 10 minutes.

5. Pour in the stock, bring to a boil, then reduce the heat and simmer, covered, for 20 minutes.

6. Remove from the heat and let cool slightly. Blend in the saucepan using a handheld blender. Stir in the milk, season with salt and pepper, then return the soup to the heat and heat until hot.

7. Ladle the soup into warm bowls, sprinkle with the croutons, and serve immediately.

HERO TIPS

It is important to let the soup to cool considerably before blending to avoid getting any hot splashes from the soup during processing.

19

ROASTED ROOT SOUP WITH GINGER

SERVES: 4-6   **PREP TIME: 20 MINS**   **COOK TIME: 45 MINS**

INGREDIENTS

1 onion
½ small rutabaga
1 sweet potato
2 carrots
1 potato
⅓ cup olive oil
2 tablespoons tomato paste
¼ teaspoon pepper
2 large garlic cloves, peeled
2 tablespoons peanut oil
two 2-inch pieces fresh ginger, sliced into thin shreds
3½ cups hot vegetable stock
½ teaspoon sea salt
crème fraîche or sour cream and coarsely chopped fresh flat-leaf parsley, to garnish

1. Preheat the oven to 375°F. Peel the onion, rutabaga, sweet potato, carrots, and potato and cut into large, even-size chunks.

2. Mix the olive oil, tomato paste, and pepper in a large bowl. Add the vegetables and the garlic and toss to coat.

3. Spread out the vegetables in a roasting pan. Roast in the preheated oven for 20 minutes, or until the garlic is soft. Remove the garlic and set aside. Roast the vegetables for an additional 10–15 minutes, until tender.

4. Meanwhile, heat the peanut oil in a skillet over high heat. Add the ginger and sauté, turning continuously, for 1–2 minutes, until crisp. Immediately remove the ginger from the skillet and drain on paper towels. Set aside and keep warm.

5. Put the garlic and the other roasted vegetables into a food processor. Process to a rough puree.

6. Pour the puree into a saucepan and add the stock. Add the salt, then simmer, stirring, for 1–2 minutes, until heated through.

7. Ladle the soup into warm serving bowls and swirl in a little crème fraîche. Top with the sizzled ginger threads and chopped parsley and serve immediately.

BEET BORSCHT SOUP

Borscht is a soup that originates from the Ukraine. It has become popular across the world, due to emigrants from Eastern Europe taking the recipe with them to elsewhere in Europe and the USA.

SERVES: 6   **PREP TIME: 15 MINS**   **COOK TIME: 1¼ HRS**

INGREDIENTS

1 onion

4 tablespoons butter

4 raw beets, cut into thin sticks, and 1 raw beet, grated

1 carrot, cut into thin batons

3 celery stalks, thinly sliced

2 tomatoes, peeled, seeded and chopped

6 cups vegetable stock

1 tablespoon white wine vinegar

1 tablespoon sugar

2 tablespoons snipped fresh dill

1¼ cups shredded green cabbage

⅔ cup sour cream

salt and pepper, to taste

crusty bread, to serve

1. Slice the onion into rings. Melt the butter in a large, heavy saucepan. Add the onion and cook over low heat, stirring occasionally, for 3–5 minutes, or until softened. Add the beet sticks, carrot, celery, and tomatoes and cook, stirring frequently, for 4–5 minutes.

2. Add the stock, vinegar, sugar, and 1 tablespoon of the dill into the saucepan. Season with salt and pepper. Bring to a boil, reduce the heat, and simmer for 35–40 minutes, or until the vegetables are tender.

3. Stir in the cabbage, cover, and simmer for 10 minutes. Stir in the grated beet, with any juices, and cook for an additional 10 minutes. Ladle into warm bowls. Top with the sour cream, sprinkle with the remaining dill, and serve with crusty bread.

HERO TIPS

Beets are rich in the compounds that safeguard our health—it is high in several important vitamins and minerals and contains antioxidants.

POTATO & CORN FRITTERS WITH RELISH

SERVES: 8

PREP TIME: 20 MINS PLUS RESTING

COOK TIME: 20 MINS

INGREDIENTS

½ cup whole-wheat flour

½ teaspoon ground coriander

½ teaspoon cumin seeds

¼ teaspoon chili powder

½ teaspoon turmeric

¼ teaspoon salt

1 egg

3 tablespoons milk

3 Yukon gold or russet potatoes

1–2 garlic cloves, crushed

4 scallions, chopped

⅓ cup corn kernels

vegetable oil, for pan-frying

ONION & TOMATO RELISH

1 onion

2 tomatoes

2 tablespoons chopped fresh cilantro

2 tablespoons chopped fresh mint

2 tablespoons lemon juice

½ teaspoon roasted cumin seeds

¼ teaspoon salt

pinch of cayenne pepper

1. To make the relish, cut the onion and tomatoes into small dice and place in a bowl with the remaining ingredients. Mix together well and let stand for at least 15 minutes before serving to let the flavors blend.

2. Place the flour in a bowl, stir in the spices and salt, and make a well in the center. Add the egg and milk and mix to form a fairly thick batter.

3. Coarsely grate the potatoes, place them in a colander, and rinse well under cold running water. Drain and squeeze dry, then stir them into the batter with the garlic, scallions, and corn kernels and mix to combine thoroughly.

4. Heat about ¼ inch of oil in a large skillet and add a few tablespoons of the batter at a time, flattening each to form a thin cake. Sauté over low heat, turning frequently, for 2–3 minutes, or until golden brown and cooked through.

5. Drain the fritters on paper towels and keep them hot while sautéing the remaining batter in the same way. Serve the potato fritters hot with the relish.

CARROT SAUSAGES & MASHED POTATOES

SERVES: 4

PREP TIME: 20 MINS PLUS CHILLING

COOK TIME: 30-35 MINS

INGREDIENTS
SAUSAGES

1 tablespoon olive oil

½ cup chopped scallions

1 garlic clove, chopped

½ fresh red chile, seeded and finely chopped

1 teaspoon ground cumin

8 carrots (1 pound), grated

½ teaspoon salt

3 tablespoons chunky peanut butter

½ cup finely chopped fresh cilantro, plus extra to garnish

2 cups fresh whole-wheat bread crumbs

all-purpose flour, for dusting

vegetable oil, for sautéing

MASHED POTATOES

8 russet or Yukon gold potatoes, chopped

3 tablespoons milk

4 tablespoons butter or margarine

salt and pepper, to taste

1. To make the sausages, heat the olive oil in a large saucepan over medium heat. Sauté the scallions, garlic, chile, and cumin for 2 minutes. Stir in the carrots and salt and mix well. Cover the pan and cook on low heat for 6–8 minutes, or until the carrot is tender.

2. Transfer the carrot mixture to a large mixing bowl and mix in the peanut butter and cilantro, making sure that the ingredients are thoroughly combined. Let the mixture cool, then mix in the bread crumbs.

3. On a floured surface, form the mixture into eight large logs. Let chill in the refrigerator for up to an hour. Heat the vegetable oil in a skillet over medium heat and sauté the sausages gently for 10 minutes, turning occasionally, until browned.

4. Meanwhile, bring a large saucepan of lightly salted water to a boil. Add the potatoes, bring back to a boil, and cook for 15–20 minutes, or until cooked through and fluffy. Transfer to a mixing bowl, add the milk and margarine, and mash the mixture thoroughly until all lumps are removed. Season with salt and pepper.

5. Place the mashed potatoes on warm plates and top with the carrot sausages. Garnish with cilantro and serve.

SWEET POTATO PANCAKES

MAKES: 4   **PREP TIME: 15 MINS**   **COOK TIME: 25 MINS**

INGREDIENTS

1 cup milk
⅓ cup all-purpose flour
½ cup chickpea (besan) flour
1 small sweet potato, grated
1 small red onion, finely chopped
vegetable oil, for frying

FILLING

5½ cups fresh baby spinach
leaves, shredded
2 tablespoons dried currants
1 tablespoon olive oil
¼ cup pine nuts
salt and pepper, to taste

1. To make the filling, put the spinach into a saucepan over medium heat. Add a splash of water and cook for about 2–3 minutes or until wilted. Turn out onto a plate, then blot firmly with paper towels to squeeze out as much water as possible. Set aside.

2. To make the pancakes, whisk together the milk, all-purpose flour, and chickpea flour in a large bowl. Stir in the sweet potato and onion, and mix thoroughly.

3. Heat a small amount of vegetable oil in a large skillet over high heat and pour one-quarter of the pancake batter into the skillet, using the back of a spoon to spread out the batter to the edges of the skillet. Sauté for 2–3 minutes on each side, turning carefully, until brown and crisp. Transfer to a warm plate lined with paper towels and make three more pancakes.

4. Return the spinach to the saucepan with the currants, olive oil, and pine nuts and put over medium heat. Season with salt and pepper and cook for a minute or until heated through. Put one-quarter of the spinach mixture onto one half of a pancake. Fold over the other half. Repeat with the remaining pancakes and serve immediately while still warm.

GET FRESH!

When you shop for root vegetables, be discerning, even if buying from a farmers' market. There is no reason why you shouldn't choose the best available yourself instead of taking what has been selected on your behalf.

Roots should feel firm and smell pleasantly fresh. Ideally, choose earth-encrusted ones; the soil acts as a protective barrier and keeps them in good condition. Once you get them home, shake off any excess soil, but resist the urge to wash it all off until you are ready to cook.

If buying plastic-wrapped roots from a supermarket, inspect them carefully for signs of bruising and make sure the flesh feels firm through the plastic.

BEET
Select: small-to-medium (large ones can be woody), leaves preferably attached, firm flesh.

Reject: spongy texture, bruises, cracks.

CARROT
Select: firm flesh, crisp when snapped.

Reject: greening around the top, cracks, whiskery rootlets, brown patches, slime, small holes (a sign of pest invasion).

CELERIAC
Select: slightly damp skin, firm flesh, heavy for size.

Reject: soft spots, bruises, brown patches.

JERUSALEM ARTICHOKE
Select: firm flesh, crisp when snapped.

Reject: spongy texture, bruises, broken or dry tips.

PARSNIP
Select: small-to-medium (large ones can be woody), firm flesh.

Reject: spongy texture, bruises, slime, cracks, sprouting at the top.

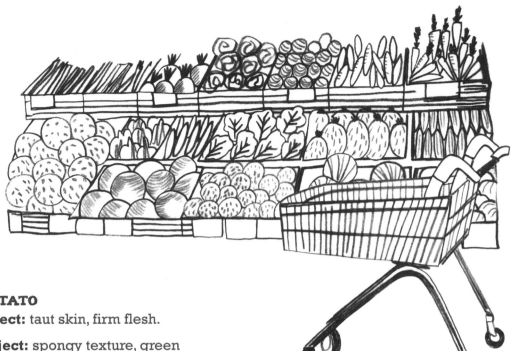

POTATO
Select: taut skin, firm flesh.

Reject: spongy texture, green patches, bruises, slime, cracks, sprouting eyes.

RADISH
Select: slightly damp skin, firm flesh, lets preferably attached.

Reject: spongy texture, bruises, cracks, sprouting at the top.

RUTABAGA
Select: small-to-medium (large ones can be woody), firm flesh, heavy for size.

Reject: spongy texture, bruises, cracks.

SWEET POTATO
Select: taut skin, firm flesh.

Reject: spongy texture, bruises, cracks.

TURNIP
Select: small-to-medium (large ones can be woody), taut skin, firm flesh.

Reject: pitted skin, spongy texture, bruises.

YAM
Select: taught skin, firm flesh. If sold in sections, the cut end should be mold-free and sealed with plastic wrap.

Reject: spongy texture, bruises, cracks, slime, mold.

31

YAM & BEEF STEW WITH COUSCOUS

SERVES: 4-6

PREP TIME: 15 MINS PLUS MARINATING

COOK TIME: 1½ HRS

INGREDIENTS

1¾ pounds boneless chuck beef

2 onions, chopped

1⅓ cups cubed yams

8 ounces new potatoes, halved

1 (15-ounce) can chickpeas, drained and rinsed

1 (14½-ounce) can diced tomatoes

1 cup red wine or water

salt and pepper, to taste

MARINADE

2 tablespoons vegetable oil

2 tablespoons chopped fresh cilantro

2 cinnamon sticks

1 tablespoon honey

1 teaspoon ground paprika

1 teaspoon ground cumin

1 teaspoon harissa paste

1 teaspoon salt

COUSCOUS

1 cup couscous

1 tablespoon coarsely chopped fresh flat-leaf parsley

1 bunch scallions, chopped

juice of 1 lemon

2 tablespoons olive oil

1. Trim the beef, cut into 1-inch pieces, and put into a large bowl. Add the marinade ingredients and stir well to combine. Cover and chill in the refrigerator for 6 hours or overnight.

2. Preheat the oven to 375°F. Transfer the meat and the marinade to a casserole dish and add the onions, yam, new potatoes, and chickpeas. Pour the tomatoes and wine over the top and stir well. Cook in the preheated oven for 1 hour.

3. Remove from the oven, stir well, and check the seasoning. If all the liquid has been absorbed, add enough water to create a generous sauce. Return the casserole to the oven and cook for an additional 30 minutes, or until the meat is tender.

4. Meanwhile, put the couscous into a bowl and pour 1 cup of boiling water of the grains. Season with salt and let stand for 5 minutes. Stir in the parsley and scallions and drizzle with the lemon juice and olive oil. Remove the cinnamon sticks from the stew and serve the stew immediately with the couscous.

BEET BURGERS IN A BUN

These wholesome, crisp beet-and-millet burgers originally hail from Australia. The tangy yogurt sauce contrasts with the sweet, earthy flavor of the vegetables.

MAKES: 5

PREP TIME: 30 MINS PLUS CHILLING

COOK TIME: 35-40 MINS

INGREDIENTS

½ cup millet (available in health food stores)

¾ cup lightly salted water

2 raw beets, shredded

⅓ cup shredded carrot

1 medium zucchini, shredded

½ cup finely chopped walnuts

2 tablespoons cider vinegar

2 tablespoons extra virgin olive oil, plus extra for sautéing

1 egg

2 tablespoons cornstarch

1 cup yogurt

2 teaspoons finely chopped garlic

5 multigrain buns, split

lettuce leaves

salt and pepper, to taste

1. Rinse and drain the millet and place in a small saucepan with the salted water. Place over medium heat, bring to a simmer, cover, and cook over low heat for 20–25 minutes, until tender. Remove from the heat and let stand for 5 minutes, covered.

2. Put the beets, carrot, zucchini, and walnuts into a large bowl. Add the millet, vinegar, oil, ½ teaspoon of salt, and ¼ teaspoon of pepper, and mix well. Add the egg and cornstarch, mix again, then chill in the refrigerator for 2 hours.

3. Put the yogurt in a fine strainer over a bowl and drain for at least 30 minutes. Stir in the garlic and season with salt and pepper.

4. Divide the beet mixture into five equal balls, then shape into five patties. Place a ridged grill pan or large skillet over medium heat and coat with oil. Add the patties and cook for about 5 minutes on each side, turning carefully, until brown.

5. Spread the buns with the yogurt sauce and place the burgers in the buns, topped with the lettuce. Serve immediately.

JERUSALEM ARTICHOKES WITH TOMATO SAUCE

Not to be confused with the globe artichoke, this ugly-looking root vegetable is actually a member of the sunflower family. Although Jerusalem artichokes can be cooked in many ways, a simple, freshly made tomato sauce is the perfect way to show them off.

SERVES: 4   **PREP TIME: 10 MINS**   **COOK TIME: 30 MINS**

INGREDIENTS

3 cups sliced Jerusalem artichokes (about 1 pound)

juice of ½ lemon

SAUCE

2 tablespoons olive oil

1 large red onion, finely chopped

2 garlic cloves, finely chopped

3 cups halved baby plum tomatoes

3 sun-dried tomatoes, chopped, or 1 tablespoon tomato paste

1 cup dry white wine

salt and pepper, to taste

2 tablespoons chopped fresh basil leaves, to garnish

1. Put the artichokes into a bowl with the lemon juice, stir to coat, then set aside until ready to cook.

2. To make the sauce, heat the oil in a skillet, add the onion, and sauté over low heat, stirring occasionally, for 5 minutes. Add the garlic and cook for an additional 2 minutes. Add the plum tomatoes, sun-dried tomatoes, and wine. Season with salt and pepper, bring to a boil, then reduce the heat and simmer, shaking the skillet occasionally, for 10 minutes.

3. Meanwhile, bring a large saucepan of lightly salted water to a boil, add the artichokes, and cook for 5–8 minutes, or until tender. Drain and transfer to a warm serving dish. Top with the tomato mixture, garnish with basil, and serve.

YAM-TOPPED BEEF CASSEROLE

SERVES: 4   **PREP TIME: 20 MINS**   **COOK TIME: 1½ HRS**

INGREDIENTS

2 tablespoons vegetable oil
2 onions, chopped
¾ cup finely chopped carrots
¾ cup finely chopped rutabaga
1 pound fresh ground beef
1 teaspoon chopped
fresh rosemary
1 tablespoon chopped
fresh parsley
1 tablespoon tomato paste
1 tablespoon all-purpose flour
1 (14½-ounce) can
diced tomatoes
1¼ cups beef stock
½ teaspoon Worcestershire
sauce
few drops hot pepper sauce,
to taste

TOPPING

2 pounds yams, cut into small
even-size pieces
4 tablespoons butter
2 leeks, thinly sliced
½ cup shredded sharp
cheddar cheese
salt and pepper, to taste

1. Heat the oil in a large skillet, add the onions, carrots, and rutabaga, and cook over high heat for 5 minutes, stirring occasionally until the onions are beginning to brown. Using a slotted spoon, transfer the vegetables to a plate. Add the beef to the skillet and brown over high heat, stirring to break up.

2. Stir in the herbs, tomato paste, and flour. Return the cooked vegetables to the skillet with the tomatoes and stock. Add the Worcestershire sauce and season with the hot pepper sauce. Bring to a boil, then reduce the heat and simmer for 30 minutes.

3. Meanwhile, to make the topping, bring a large saucepan of lightly salted water to a boil. Add the yams and cook for 15–20 minutes, or until tender. Drain and return to the pan with the butter and mash thoroughly. Season with salt and pepper. Preheat the oven to 400°F.

4. Transfer the meat mixture to a baking dish, top with the mashed yams, and spread evenly over the meat. Sprinkle the leeks over the top, then sprinkle with the cheese. Bake in the preheated oven for 35–40 minutes, or until golden. Serve immediately.

HOME FROM WORK & HUNGRY

Get Prepped! 42

Carrot & Orange Stir-Fry 44

New Potato, Feta & Herb Frittata 46

Yam, Rutabaga & Mushroom Hash 48

Jerusalem Artichoke & Hazelnut Gratin 50

Celeriac Salad with Crab 52

Lamb & Turnip Stew 54

Raw Beet & Pecan Salad 56

Parsnip Layered Casserole 58

Potato & Radish Salad 60

Baked Potatoes, Broccoli & Peanuts 62

Pan-Cooked Tuna with Radish Relish 64

Stir-Fried Chicken & Rutabaga 66

GET PREPPED!

Some root vegetables may seem daunting to prepare, but it's easy when you know how. Follow our simple guide to preparing beets and celeriac.

1. To prepare a beet, remove the leaves and stem with a knife. Leave about 1 inch of the stem intact.

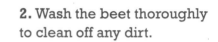

2. Wash the beet thoroughly to clean off any dirt.

3. Wear rubber gloves when peeling the beet to avoid staining your hands.

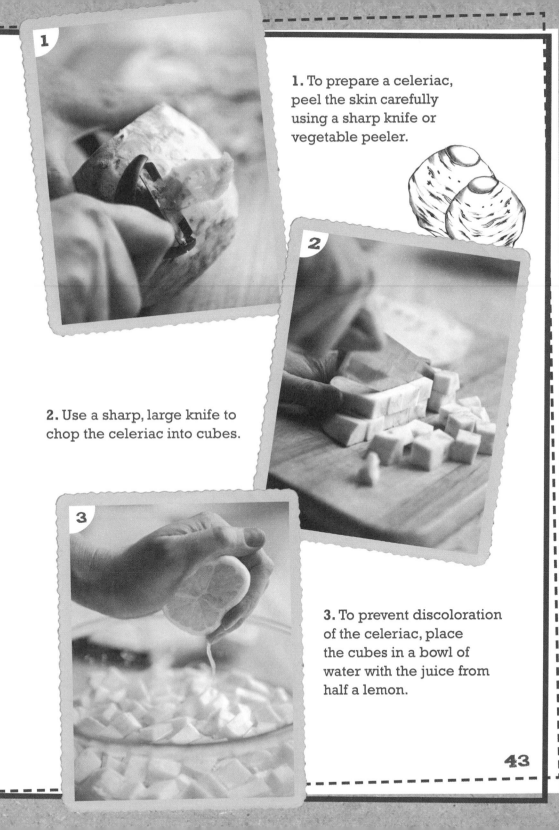

1. To prepare a celeriac, peel the skin carefully using a sharp knife or vegetable peeler.

2. Use a sharp, large knife to chop the celeriac into cubes.

3. To prevent discoloration of the celeriac, place the cubes in a bowl of water with the juice from half a lemon.

CARROT & ORANGE STIR-FRY

This is a quick and healthy dinner to put together after a busy day at work. The crisp vegetables combine deliciously with the sweet-and-sour sauce.

SERVES: 4   **PREP TIME: 10 MINS**   **COOK TIME: 10 MINS**

INGREDIENTS

2 tablespoons sunflower oil
8 carrots, shredded
2½ leeks, shredded
2 oranges, peeled and segmented
2 tablespoons ketchup
1 tablespoon demerara or other raw sugar
2 tablespoons light soy sauce
⅔ cup chopped peanuts

1. Heat the oil in a large wok. Add the carrots and leeks to the wok and stir-fry for 2–3 minutes, or until the vegetables are just soft.

2. Add the oranges to the wok and heat through gently, making sure that you do not break up the orange segments as you stir the mixture.

3. Mix together the ketchup, sugar, and soy sauce in a small bowl.

4. Add the ketchup mixture to the wok and stir-fry for an additional 2 minutes.

5. Transfer the stir-fry to warm serving bowls and sprinkle with the peanuts. Serve immediately.

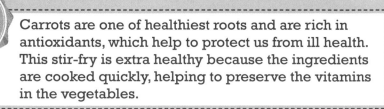

HERO TIPS

Carrots are one of healthiest roots and are rich in antioxidants, which help to protect us from ill health. This stir-fry is extra healthy because the ingredients are cooked quickly, helping to preserve the vitamins in the vegetables.

NEW POTATO, FETA & HERB FRITTATA

SERVES: 4   **PREP TIME: 10 MINS**   **COOK TIME: 35 MINS**

INGREDIENTS

8 ounces new potatoes, scrubbed

3 ounces baby spinach leaves

5 eggs

1 tablespoon chopped fresh dill, plus extra to garnish

1 tablespoon snipped fresh chives, plus extra to garnish

¾ cup crumbled feta cheese

½ tablespoon butter

1 tablespoon olive oil

salt and pepper, to taste

1. Bring a saucepan of lightly salted water to a boil, add the potatoes, bring back to a boil, and cook for 25 minutes, until tender. Place the spinach in a colander and drain the potatoes over the top to wilt the spinach. Set aside until cool enough to handle.

2. Cut the potatoes lengthwise into ¼-inch-thick slices. Squeeze the excess water from the spinach leaves. Preheat the broiler to high.

3. Lightly beat together the eggs, dill, and chives. Season with pepper and add ½ cup of the cheese. Heat the butter and oil in an 8-inch skillet until melted and foaming. Add the potato slices and spinach and cook, stirring, for 1 minute. Pour the egg-and-cheese mixture over the top.

4. Cook, stirring, over medium heat for 1 minute, until half set, then continue to cook for an additional 2–3 minutes, without stirring, until set and golden brown underneath. Sprinkle the remaining cheese over the top, place under the preheated broiler, and cook for 2 minutes, until golden brown on top. Serve hot or cold, sprinkled with chives and dill.

YAM, RUTABAGA & MUSHROOM HASH

A hearty hash that combines tastes and textures for a great breakfast or brunch dish. A few eggs broken into the mixture during the last few minutes of cooking makes a really tasty treat!

SERVES: 4　　　　**PREP TIME: 15 MINS**　　　　**COOK TIME: 30 MINS**

INGREDIENTS

3 tablespoons olive oil
3 cups diced yam
2 cups diced rutabaga
1 onion, chopped
6 ounces bacon rashers, sliced
3½ cups sliced mushrooms
4 eggs
salt and pepper, to taste
chopped fresh parsley, to garnish

1. Heat the oil in a large, lidded skillet over high heat. Add the yam and rutabaga, stir in the oil to coat, and season with salt and pepper. Cook, stirring occasionally, for 10–15 minutes, or until the vegetables are just turning golden and soft.

2. Add the onion and bacon, stir well, and continue to cook for 5 minutes, until the onion is soft and the bacon is cooked. Stir in the mushrooms, cover the pan, and cook for an additional 5 minutes.

3. Make four indentations in the mixture and carefully break an egg into each one. Cover the pan and cook for an additional 3–4 minutes, or until the egg whites are firm but the yolks are still soft. Garnish with parsley and serve immediately.

HERO TIPS

The yam is a versatile vegetable—it can be roasted, fried, grilled, broiled, and boiled, and when grated, it can be used in desserts, too.

JERUSALEM ARTICHOKE & HAZELNUT GRATIN

SERVES: 4　　　　**PREP TIME: 15 MINS**　　　　**COOK TIME: 45 MINS**

INGREDIENTS

1¾ pounds Jerusalem artichokes

squeeze of lemon juice

¼ cup skinned hazelnuts, coarsely chopped

1 cup coarse ciabatta bread crumbs

2 tablespoons butter, plus extra for greasing

salt and pepper, to taste

steamed green beans, to serve

GARLIC CREAM

1 cup heavy cream

7 large garlic cloves, lightly crushed

sliver of lemon peel

squeeze of lemon juice

1. To make the garlic cream, heat the cream, garlic, and lemon peel in a saucepan over medium heat, then simmer for about 5 minutes, until slightly reduced. Remove from the heat and let stand in a warm place.

2. Peel the artichokes, dropping them into water with a squeeze of lemon juice. Cut in half if they are large. Place in a steamer basket set over a saucepan of boiling water and steam for 8–10 minutes, until just tender at the edges. Let cool, then slice thickly.

3. Strain the garlic cream into a small bowl. Add the lemon juice and season.

4. Preheat the oven to 375°F. Grease a 2-quart baking dish with butter. Arrange half the artichoke slices in the bottom of the prepared dish. Season with salt and pepper. Sprinkle with the nuts, then top with the remaining artichokes and a little more seasoning.

5. Pour the warm garlic cream over the vegetables. Sprinkle with the bread crumbs and dot with the butter.

6. Bake in the preheated oven for 30–35 minutes, until the artichokes are tender and the topping is golden and bubbling. Serve hot with steamed green beans.

CELERIAC SALAD WITH CRAB

SERVES: 4

**PREP TIME: 15-20 MINS   COOK TIME: 2 MINS
PLUS CHILLING**

INGREDIENTS

1 head of celeriac, grated

juice of 1 lemon

9 ounces fresh white crabmeat

chopped fresh dill or parsley, to garnish

mixed salad greens, to serve

MUSTARD-MAYONNAISE DRESSING

⅔ cup mayonnaise

1 tablespoon Dijon mustard

1½ teaspoons white wine vinegar

2 tablespoons capers in brine, well rinsed

salt and white pepper, to taste

1. To make the dressing, put the mayonnaise in a bowl. Add the mustard, vinegar, and capers, season with salt and white pepper, and beat together— the mixture should be piquant with a strong mustard flavor. Cover and chill until required.

2. Bring a large saucepan of salted water to a rolling boil. Add the grated celeriac and lemon juice to the water and blanch for 1½–2 minutes, or until it is just slightly tender. Rinse the celeriac well, then put it under cold running water to stop the cooking process. Use your hands to squeeze out the excess moisture, then pat the celeriac dry with paper towels or a clean dish towel.

3. Stir the celeriac into the dressing, along with the crabmeat. Taste and adjust the seasoning, if necessary. Cover and chill for at least 30 minutes.

4. When ready to serve, spoon into bowls with the mixed salad greens and garnish with dill or parsley.

HERO TIPS

Celeriac is a root vegetable variety of celery, which accounts for its similarity in flavor. It is also delicious when mashed, as an alternative to potato.

LAMB & TURNIP STEW

SERVES: 4-6　　　　**PREP TIME: 15-20 MINS**　　**COOK TIME: 1¼ HRS**

INGREDIENTS

3 tablespoons butter

2 tablespoons sunflower oil, plus extra as needed

2 pounds boned shoulder of lamb, trimmed and cut into large chunks, any bones reserved

2 shallots, finely chopped

1 tablespoon sugar

4 cups lamb stock

2 tablespoons tomato paste

1 bouquet garni, with several parsley and thyme sprigs, 1 bay leaf, and 1 small rosemary sprig tied together

8 new potatoes, scrubbed and halved, if large

4 young turnips, quartered

12 baby carrots, scrubbed

1 cup frozen peas

salt and pepper, to taste

chopped fresh flat-leaf parsley, to garnish

baguette, to serve

1. Melt 2 tablespoons of the butter with the oil in a large skillet over medium heat. Add the lamb, in batches to avoid overcrowding the pan, and sauté, stirring, until browned on all sides, adding extra oil, if necessary. Transfer the meat to a large casserole.

2. Melt the remaining butter with the fat left in the skillet. Add the shallots and stir for 3 minutes, or until beginning to soften. Sprinkle with the sugar, increase the heat, and continue stirring until the shallots caramelize, being careful that they do not burn. Transfer to a casserole dish and remove any charred sediment from the bottom of the skillet. Add half of the stock to the skillet and bring to a boil, then transfer the mixture to the casserole dish.

3. Add the remaining stock, tomato paste, bouquet garni, and bones, if any, to the casserole. Season with salt and pepper. Cover and bring to a boil. Reduce the heat and simmer for 45 minutes.

4. Add the potatoes, turnips, and carrots and continue simmering for 15 minutes. Add the peas, then uncover and simmer for an additional 5–10 minutes, or until the meat and all the vegetables are tender. Remove and discard the bones, if used, and the bouquet garni. Taste and adjust the seasoning, if necessary. Garnish with parsley and serve with a baguette.

RAW BEET & PECAN SALAD

Originally grown just for its leaves, beet is also a rich source of folic acid and iron. Its strong, vibrant color makes it a great addition to salads and soups because it adds real visual appeal to these dishes.

SERVES: 4　　　　**PREP TIME: 10 MINS**　　　　**COOK TIME: NONE**

INGREDIENTS

3 fresh beets, shredded

8 radishes, thinly sliced

2 scallions, finely chopped

3 tablespoons coarsely chopped pecans

8 red endive leaves or Boston lettuce leaves

DRESSING

2 tablespoons extra virgin olive oil

1 tablespoon balsamic vinegar

2 teaspoons creamed horseradish sauce

salt and pepper, to taste

1. Combine the beets, radishes, scallions, and pecans in a bowl and toss well to mix evenly.

2. Place all the dressing ingredients in a small bowl and whisk lightly with a fork. Season with salt and pepper and pour the dressing over the vegetables in the bowl, tossing to coat evenly.

3. Arrange the endive or lettuce leaves on a serving plate and spoon the salad over them.

4. Serve the salad cold on its own or as an accompaniment to main dishes.

56

PARSNIP LAYERED CASSEROLE

SERVES: 4-6　　　　**PREP TIME: 20 MINS**　　　**COOK TIME: 1 HR**

INGREDIENTS

3 tablespoons olive oil

5 parsnips, thinly sliced

1 teaspoon fresh thyme leaves

1 teaspoon sugar

1¼ cups heavy cream

5 tomatoes, thinly sliced

1 teaspoon dried oregano

1⅓ cups shredded cheddar cheese

salt and pepper, to taste

1. Preheat the oven to 350°F.

2. Heat the oil in a skillet over medium heat, add the parsnips, thyme, and sugar, season with salt and pepper, and cook, stirring frequently, for 6–8 minutes, until golden and softened.

3. Spread half the parsnips over the bottom of a gratin dish. Pour over half the cream, then arrange half the tomatoes in an even layer across the parsnips. Season with salt and pepper and sprinkle with half the oregano. Sprinkle with half the cheddar cheese. Top with the remaining parsnips and tomatoes. Sprinkle with the remaining oregano, season with salt and pepper, and pour over the remaining cream. Sprinkle with the remaining cheese.

4. Cover with aluminum foil and bake in the preheated oven for 40 minutes, or until the parsnips are tender. Remove the foil and return to the oven for an additional 5–10 minutes, until the top is golden and bubbling. Serve immediately.

58

POTATO & RADISH SALAD

This salad is based on a traditional Italian recipe, known as Country Salad, from the province of Trento. They also sometimes serve this with cubes of Italian cheese added, such as Grana Padano.

SERVES: 4

PREP TIME: 20 MINS PLUS RESTING

COOK TIME: 35 MINS

INGREDIENTS

12 ounces new potatoes

1½ cups small cauliflower florets

¼ cup extra virgin olive oil, plus extra if needed

1½ tablespoons red wine vinegar, plus extra if needed

1 cup bite-size green bean pieces

4 scallions, finely chopped

1 radish, thinly sliced

3 cups baby spinach leaves

2 tablespoons toasted pine nuts

2 tablespoons raisins or golden raisins

salt and pepper, to taste

radicchio leaves and ciabatta bread, to serve

1. Bring two saucepans of lightly salted water to a boil. Add the potatoes to one pan, bring back to a boil, and cook for 20–25 minutes, until tender. Add the cauliflower florets to the other pan, bring back to a boil, and cook for 5 minutes, or until tender-crisp.

2. Meanwhile, put the oil and vinegar into a serving bowl, season with salt and pepper, and whisk together.

3. Use a slotted spoon to remove the cauliflower florets from the pan, shaking off the excess water, and stir them into the dressing in the bowl.

4. Drop the beans into the cauliflower cooking water, bring back to a boil, and cook for 5 minutes, or until tender-crisp. Drain well, then stir into the serving bowl.

5. Drain the potatoes and cool slightly under cold running water. Peel and cut into bite-size pieces, then stir into the dressing together with

the scallions and radish. Make sure all the vegetables are coated with dressing, then set aside for at least 1 hour.

6. When ready to serve, line a plate with radicchio leaves. Stir the spinach into the serving bowl and add extra oil, vinegar, and salt and pepper, if desired. Stir in the pine nuts and raisins.

7. Spoon the salad onto the radicchio leaves, adding any dressing left in the bowl. Serve with plenty of ciabatta bread to mop up the dressing.

BAKED POTATOES, BROCCOLI & PEANUTS

SERVES: 4   **PREP TIME: 15 MINS**   **COOK TIME: 50 MINS**

INGREDIENTS

1 pound new potatoes, sliced
1 tablespoon olive oil
½ small onion, finely chopped
1¾ cups coconut milk
½ cup chunky peanut butter
1 tablespoon soy sauce
2 teaspoons sugar
½ teaspoon crushed red pepper flakes
3 cups broccoli florets
½ cup unsalted peanuts
2 teaspoons margarine, melted
salt and pepper, to taste

1. Preheat the oven to 375°F.

2. Bring a large saucepan of lightly salted water to a boil. Add the potatoes, bring back to a boil, and cook for 8–10 minutes, or until slightly softened. Drain and set aside.

3. Heat the oil in a saucepan over medium heat. Sauté the onion for 2 minutes, then stir in the coconut milk, peanut butter, soy sauce, sugar, and red pepper flakes. Bring to a boil and stir well to make sure the ingredients are well combined. Reduce the heat and simmer for 5 minutes.

4. Meanwhile, place the broccoli in a steamer and lightly steam for 4–5 minutes, or until just tender.

5. Stir the broccoli and peanuts into the sauce, season, and transfer to a wide, square baking dish.

6. Cover the mixture with the cooked potato slices, dot with the melted margarine, and season with pepper. Bake in the preheated oven for 20–25 minutes, or until the potatoes are golden. Let cool for 5 minutes before serving.

3

5

6

63

PAN-COOKED TUNA WITH RADISH RELISH

Borrowing from the Japanese tradition of pickling vegetables, the radishes and cucumber are marinated in a delicious mix of sweet and sour, which goes particularly well with the tuna.

SERVES: 4

PREP TIME: 15 MINS PLUS MARINATING

COOK TIME: 10 MINS

INGREDIENTS

4 (5-ounce) tuna steaks
1 tablespoon sesame seeds
cooked rice, to serve (optional)

MARINADE

2 tablespoons dark soy sauce
2 tablespoons sunflower oil
1 tablespoon sesame oil
1 tablespoon rice vinegar
1 teaspoon grated fresh ginger

RELISH

½ cucumber, peeled
1 bunch red radishes, trimmed

1. Place the tuna steaks in a dish and sprinkle with the sesame seeds, pressing them in with the back of a spoon so they stick to the fish.

2. To make the marinade, whisk together all the ingredients. Transfer 3 tablespoons of the marinade to a medium bowl. Pour the remaining marinade over the fish, turning each steak to coat lightly. Cover and chill for 1 hour.

3. Slice the cucumber and radishes thinly and add to the marinade in the bowl. Toss the vegetables to coat, then cover and chill.

4. Heat a large, heavy skillet over high heat. Add the fish and cook for 3–4 minutes on each side, depending on the thickness of the salmon. Serve immediately with the radish relish and rice (if using).

HERO TIPS

Use a ridged grill pan to create attractive dark stripes on the tuna steaks or cook the steaks on a grill on a barbecue.

STIR-FRIED CHICKEN & RUTABAGA

SERVES: 4

PREP TIME: 15 MINS PLUS MARINATING

COOK TIME: 15-20 MINS

INGREDIENTS

4 (4-ounce) skinless, boneless chicken breasts

3 tablespoons vegetable oil

½ rutabaga, finely shredded

3 red, orange, or yellow bell peppers, seeded and cut into thin strips

4 fine dried egg noodle nests

chopped fresh cilantro, to garnish

MARINADE

1 red chile, seeded and finely chopped

1-inch piece fresh ginger, grated

2 garlic cloves, finely chopped

2 tablespoons ketchup

2 tablespoons Chinese plum sauce

2 tablespoons dark soy sauce

1. Cut the chicken breasts into 1-inch pieces and place in a bowl. Add all the marinade ingredients and stir to coat the chicken. Cover and let stand at room temperature for 15 minutes, or chill in the refrigerator for up to 3 hours.

2. Heat 1 tablespoon of the oil in a wok or large skillet, then add the rutabaga and bell peppers. Cook, stirring occasionally, for 8–10 minutes, or until the vegetables begin to soften. Using a slotted spoon, transfer to a warm plate.

3. Heat the remaining oil in the wok and add the chicken and marinade. Cook, for 4–5 minutes, stirring, or until the chicken is cooked through and shows no traces of pink. Return the vegetables to the wok and continue to cook, stirring occasionally, until heated through.

4. Meanwhile, bring a small saucepan of water to a boil and add the noodles. Bring back to a boil, then simmer for 3 minutes, or according to the package directions, until the noodles are cooked. Drain and divide among four serving plates. Top with the chicken and vegetables and garnish with cilantro. Serve immediately.

LET ME ENTERTAIN YOU

Sweet Potato Ravioli with Sage Butter 70

Roasted Beet Packages 72

Putting Down Roots 74

Caramelized Rutabaga & Ham Pie 76

Potato Gnocchi with Walnut Pesto 78

Carrot Upside-Down Tart 80

Spiced Parsnip Gratin with Ginger Cream 82

Beet, Lobster & Spinach Risotto 84

Baked Root Vegetable & Rosemary Cake 86

Slow-Cooked Potato Stew 88

Pork Braised with Celeriac & Orange 90

What's Cooking? 92

Creamed Chicken with Jerusalem Artichokes ... 94

Sweet Potato Curry with Lentils 96

SWEET POTATO RAVIOLI WITH SAGE BUTTER

SERVES: 4

PREP TIME: 30 MINS PLUS CHILLING

COOK TIME: 30 MINS

INGREDIENTS

3¼ cups all-purpose flour

4 eggs, beaten

semolina, for dusting

salt

FILLING

3 sweet potatoes

3 tablespoons olive oil

1 large onion, finely chopped

1 garlic clove, crushed

1 teaspoon chopped fresh thyme

2 tablespoons honey

salt and pepper, to taste

SAGE BUTTER

4 tablespoons butter

1 bunch of fresh sage leaves, finely chopped, plus extra leaves to garnish

1. To make the pasta dough, sift the flour into a large bowl or food processor. Add the eggs and bring together the mixture or process to make a soft but not sticky dough. Turn out onto a work surface lightly dusted with semolina and knead for 4–5 minutes, until smooth. Cover with plastic wrap and chill in the refrigerator for at least 30 minutes.

2. For the filling, peel the sweet potatoes and cut into chunks. Cook in a saucepan of boiling water for 20 minutes, or until tender. Drain and mash.

3. Heat the oil in a skillet over medium heat, add the onion, and cook, stirring frequently, for 4–5 minutes, until softened but not browned. Stir the onion into the mashed sweet potatoes and add the garlic and thyme. Drizzle with the honey and season with salt and pepper. Set aside.

4. Using a pasta machine, roll the pasta out to a thickness of about $\frac{1}{32}$ inch (or use a rolling pin on a work surface lightly dusted with semolina).

5. Cut the pasta in half. Place teaspoonfuls of the filling at evenly spaced intervals across half of the pasta. Brush around the filling with a small amount of water and cover with the second half of the pasta. Press lightly around the filling to seal and cut into squares with a sharp knife or pastry wheel. Lay the ravioli out on a sheet of wax paper that has been lightly dusted with semolina.

6. Bring a large saucepan of salted water to a boil and drop in the ravioli. Cook for 2–3 minutes, until the pasta rises to the surface and is tender but still firm to the bite.

7. Meanwhile, for the sage butter, melt the butter with the chopped sage in a small saucepan over low heat.

8. Drain the ravioli and immediately toss with the sage butter. Serve immediately, garnished with sage leaves.

ROASTED BEET PACKAGES

SERVES: 4

PREP TIME: 15 MINS PLUS COOLING

COOK TIME: 2 HRS

INGREDIENTS

olive oil, for greasing and tossing

8 small beets, halved

4 fresh thyme sprigs

¼ cup grated fresh horseradish, or grated horseradish from a jar

1 stick unsalted butter

sea salt flakes and pepper, to taste

arugula leaves, to serve

POLENTA

3½ cups water

1¼ cups polenta or cornmeal

1 teaspoon salt

1. To make the polenta, bring the water to a boil in a large saucepan. Slowly add the polenta and salt, stirring continuously. Simmer, stirring frequently, according to the package directions, until the mixture comes away from the side of the pan.

2. Grease a small roasting pan. Transfer the polenta to the pan, level the surface, and let cool.

3. Preheat the oven to 375°F. Toss the beets with enough oil to coat.

4. Place four beet halves and a thyme sprig on a square of thick aluminum foil. Season. Wrap in a loose package, sealing the edges. Repeat with the remaining beets and place on a baking sheet.

5. Roast in the preheated oven for about 1 hour or until just tender.

6. Meanwhile, mash the horseradish with the butter, ½ teaspoon of salt, and ¼ teaspoon of pepper. Roll into a log, using a piece of plastic wrap, and chill in the refrigerator.

7. Preheat the broiler to high. Slice the polenta into four neat rectangles. Spread out in a broiler pan, brush with oil, and cook under a hot broiler for 5 minutes. Turn and broil for an additional 3 minutes, until crisp.

8. Arrange the polenta on serving plates. Place the beet and a slice of horseradish butter on top. Add a handful of arugula to each plate and serve immediately.

PUTTING DOWN ROOTS

Even if you have only limited experience and space, you can still grow your own root vegetables. If you have just a balcony or patio, grow them in deep soil mix-filled containers, such as tall terra-cotta flowerpots or even a bucket. By selecting colorful types, your veggie plants may even be mistaken for beautiful ornamentals. Ideally, choose a space that gets sun for most of the day.

WHAT TO GROW

Roots that take forever to mature—rutabagas and parsnips, for example—are not the best choice. If you are short of time, don't get carried away with attention-seeking plants, such as celeriac and salsify. Think about what you like to eat. Radishes may be easy to grow, but are pointless if no one wants to eat them. Ultimately, it makes sense to stick to quick-growing cultivars that are hard to find in grocery stores and have a high yield-to-space ratio.

Beet is a good no-nonsense choice for a beginner and has the advantage that you can also eat the leaves. The roots are fast growing, can be eaten at any size, and come in dazzling colors. Impress your guests with golden or pink-and-white candy-striped cultivars. Sow in early spring for a midsummer harvest, and continue sowing monthly

until midsummer. The beet seed is actually a fruit containing two or three seeds. Several seedlings may emerge from each fruit, forming little clusters that need thinning. Use the smallest in salads and let the strongest continue to grow. They will be ready in 9–12 weeks. The last roots of the season may tough it out over winter if covered with straw or a horticultural cover, if you can store it in a frost-free place.

Carrots are another rewarding crop, and one of the tastiest. There is a great choice of shapes, sizes, and colors: blunt or wedge shape, dumpy or long, and if you don't like orange, go for white, purple, or yellow. There are plenty to choose from in the catalogs. Carrots are fussy about soil. Long cultivars may become stunted in shallow soil, but short round ones will do well. Choose a tall containers for cultivars with long roots. Sow carrots in late winter for a late-spring harvest. You can start pulling them once they are big enough to eat.

CARAMELIZED RUTABAGA & HAM PIE

SERVES: 4   **PREP TIME: 10 MINS**   **COOK TIME: 1 HR**

INGREDIENTS

1¼ pounds cooked ham, cubed

6 tablespoons butter

2 onions, chopped

3 cups cubed rutabaga

1 teaspoon chopped fresh sage

3 tablespoons all-purpose flour, plus extra for dusting

2½ cups milk

12 ounces ready-to-bake puff pastry, thawed if frozen

beaten egg, to glaze

salt and pepper, to taste

1. Put the ham into a large bowl and set aside. Melt 4 tablespoons of the butter in a large skillet over medium heat. Add the onions, rutabaga, and sage and season with salt and pepper. Stir well and cook over medium–high heat for 35–40 minutes, occasionally turning over the pieces with a wide spatula, until golden brown.

2. Meanwhile, melt the remaining butter in a small saucepan over medium heat. Add the flour and cook, stirring, for 1–2 minutes. Gradually add the milk, stirring, to make a smooth sauce. Remove from the heat and season with salt and pepper.

3. Preheat the oven to 425°F. Roll out the pastry on a lightly floured surface to a rectangle slightly larger than the top of a 10½ x 7-inch pie dish.

4. When the vegetables are caramelized, add to the bowl with the ham, then add the white sauce, stirring gently to combine. Transfer the mixture to a pie dish, brush the rim with the beaten egg, and then lay the pastry over the filling. Press the pastry to the rim, then trim off the excess and cut out shapes to decorate the top, if desired. Brush the pastry with the beaten egg and cook in the oven for 15–20 minutes, or until the pastry is puffed and golden. Serve immediately.

POTATO GNOCCHI WITH WALNUT PESTO

SERVES: 4　　　　**PREP TIME: 30 MINS**　　　　**COOK TIME: 45 MINS**

INGREDIENTS

4 russet potatoes,
washed but not peeled

⅔ cup freshly grated
Parmesan cheese

1 egg, beaten

1⅔ cups all-purpose flour,
plus extra for dusting

salt and pepper, to taste

WALNUT PESTO

1 cup fresh flat-leaf parsley,
chopped

2 tablespoons capers,
rinsed and chopped

2 garlic cloves, chopped

¾ cup extra virgin olive oil

¾ cup walnut pieces

½ cup freshly grated
Parmesan cheese

salt and pepper, to taste

1. Bring a large saucepan of lightly salted water to a boil. Add the potatoes, bring back to a boil, and cook for 30–35 minutes, until tender. Drain well and let cool slightly.

2. Meanwhile, to make the pesto, put the parsley, capers, and garlic into a mortar with the oil and walnuts, then season with salt and pepper. Pound to a coarse paste using a pestle. Add the cheese and stir well.

3. When the potatoes are just cool enough to handle, peel off the skins and pass the flesh through a strainer into a large bowl, or press through a potato ricer. While still hot, season well with salt and pepper and add the cheese.

4. Beat in the egg and sift in the flour. Lightly mix together, then turn out onto a lightly floured work surface. Lightly knead until the mixture becomes a smooth dough. If it is too sticky, add a little more flour.

5. Using your hands, roll out the dough on a lightly floured work surface into a long log.

6. Cut the log into 1-inch pieces and gently press each piece with a fork to give the traditional ridged effect of gnocchi. Transfer the pieces to a floured baking sheet and cover with a clean dish towel.

7. Bring a large saucepan of water to a boil, add the gnocchi, in small batches, and cook for 1–2 minutes.

8. Remove with a slotted spoon and transfer to a warm dish to keep warm while you cook the remaining gnocchi. Serve the gnocchi on warm plates, topped with a good spoonful of the pesto.

CARROT UPSIDE-DOWN TART

SERVES: 4   **PREP TIME: 15 MINS**   **COOK TIME: 45 MINS**

INGREDIENTS

12 young carrots
(about 1¼ pounds),
cut into 1-inch chunks

2 tablespoons honey

2 tablespoons butter

1 small bunch fresh thyme,
chopped

12 ounces ready-to-bake
puff pastry, thawed if frozen

all-purpose flour, for dusting

salt and pepper, to taste

1. Bring a large saucepan of lightly salted water to a boil. Add the carrots, bring back to a boil, and cook for 10–15 minutes, until just tender. Drain, toss with the honey, butter, and thyme, and season with salt and pepper.

2. Preheat the oven to 400°F. Spoon the carrots over the bottom of an 8-inch tart pan or round cake pan with a depth of about 1¼ inches. Roast in the preheated oven for 15 minutes, or until the carrots are caramelized. Remove the pan from the oven but leave the oven on.

3. Roll out the pastry on a floured work surface into a circle large enough to fit the pan and provide a ¾-inch overlap. Lay the pastry carefully over the carrots and tuck the edges down between the carrots and the side of the pan to make a border. Bake in the oven for 15 minutes, or until the pastry is puffed and golden.

4. Remove the tart from the oven and turn the pan over onto a plate to release.

5. Cut the tart into slices and serve immediately.

SPICED PARSNIP GRATIN WITH GINGER CREAM

This is a deceptively easy recipe to make, but it looks and tastes really impressive, so is ideal for dinner parties. Most of the work is done in the oven, leaving you free to prepare the rest of the meal.

SERVES: 4   **PREP TIME: 15 MINS**   **COOK TIME: 40 MINS**

INGREDIENTS

butter, for greasing

3 large parsnips (about 1¾ pounds), thinly sliced

2 cups heavy cream

1 cup vegetable stock

1 garlic clove, crushed

1-inch piece fresh ginger, coarsely chopped and crushed in a garlic press

¼ teaspoon freshly ground white pepper

⅛ teaspoon freshly grated nutmeg, plus extra to garnish

sea salt, to taste

snipped chives, to garnish

1. Lightly grease a large gratin dish. Place the parsnips in a steamer basket set over a saucepan of boiling water. Steam for 3 minutes, until barely tender, shaking halfway through cooking. Transfer to the prepared dish and lightly season with salt.

2. Preheat the oven to 350°F. Gently heat the cream and stock in a saucepan with the garlic and ginger. Do not let the mixture boil. Add the pepper and nutmeg and season with sea salt.

3. Pour the hot cream mixture over the parsnips. Cover the dish with aluminum foil and bake in the preheated oven for 20 minutes, with an oven pan underneath to catch any drips.

4. Remove the foil and bake for an additional 15–20 minutes, until golden on top.

5. Sprinkle with a little more nutmeg and some chives and serve immediately.

BEET, LOBSTER & SPINACH RISOTTO

SERVES: 4   **PREP TIME: 15 MINS**   **COOK TIME: 30 MINS**

INGREDIENTS

6 ⅓ cups vegetable stock or chicken stock

2 tablespoons butter

2 tablespoons olive oil

1 small onion, diced

1½ cups risotto rice

½ cup dry white wine

5 small raw beets, grated

1 teaspoon grated horseradish

juice of ½ lemon

6 cups baby leaf spinach

8 ounces ready-to-eat lobster meat or crabmeat

¾ cup freshly grated Parmesan cheese

salt and pepper, to taste

crème fraîche, to serve

1. Bring the stock to a boil in a large saucepan, then simmer over low heat. Meanwhile, heat the butter and oil in a separate large saucepan over medium heat, add the onion, and sauté for 3 minutes. Add the rice and stir to coat with the butter and oil. Cook for an additional 2 minutes. Add the wine and simmer for 2 minutes, or until absorbed.

2. Add the beets and stir well. Add two ladles of hot stock to the pan, then cover and cook for 2 minutes, or until absorbed. Stir well and add another ladle of stock. Stir continuously until the stock is absorbed, then add another ladle. Continue adding the stock, one ladle at a time, until it has all been absorbed and the rice is almost cooked.

3. Stir in the horseradish and lemon juice, then add the spinach and season with salt and pepper. Divide among warm bowls, top with the lobster meat and cheese, and serve immediately, accompanied by the crème fraîche.

BAKED ROOT VEGETABLE & ROSEMARY CAKE

This is an unusual way to serve a varied selection of root vegetables and it is subtly flavored with rosemary and lemon to make something really special.

SERVES: 4   **PREP TIME: 15-20 MINS**   **COOK TIME: 1 HR**

INGREDIENTS

olive oil, for greasing
3 parsnips, shredded
5 carrots, shredded
½ head of celeriac, shredded
1 onion, roughly grated
2 tablespoons chopped fresh rosemary
3 tablespoons lemon juice
salt and pepper, to taste
rosemary sprigs, to garnish

1. Preheat the oven to 375°F. Grease an 8-inch round cake pan and line with parchment paper.

2. Place the parsnip, carrot, and celeriac in separate, small bowls.

3. Mix together the onion, rosemary, and lemon juice in a small bowl. Add one-third of the onion mixture to each vegetable bowl, season with salt and pepper, and stir to mix evenly.

4. Spoon the parsnips into the prepared pan, spreading evenly and pressing down lightly. Top with the carrots, press lightly, then add the celeriac.

5. Top the cake with a piece of lightly oiled aluminum foil and press down to flatten the contents. Tuck the foil over the edges of the pan to seal. Place on a baking sheet and bake in the preheated oven for about 1 hour, or until tender.

6. Remove the foil and turn out the cake onto a warm plate. Let cool for 5 minutes and then slice and serve, garnished with rosemary sprigs.

SLOW-COOKED POTATO STEW

SERVES: 4   **PREP TIME: 20 MINS**   **COOK TIME: 1 HR**

INGREDIENTS

6 Yukon gold, white round, or red-skinned potatoes, cut into 1-inch cubes

2 tablespoons butter

2 tablespoons olive oil

2 ounces pancetta or bacon, diced

1 onion, finely chopped

1 garlic clove, finely chopped

1 celery stalk, finely chopped

1 (14½-ounce) can diced tomatoes

2 tablespoons tomato paste

brown sugar, to taste

1 tablespoon chopped fresh marjoram

½ cup vegetable stock

salt and pepper, to taste

1. Parboil the potatoes in a saucepan of lightly salted boiling water for 5 minutes. Drain and set aside.

2. Melt the butter with the oil in a saucepan. Add the pancetta, onion, garlic, and celery and cook over low heat, stirring occasionally, for 5 minutes, until softened. Stir in the tomatoes, tomato paste, sugar, marjoram, and stock and season with salt and pepper. Increase the heat to medium and bring to a boil. Gently stir in the potatoes, reduce the heat to low, cover, and simmer, stirring occasionally, for 45–50 minutes, until the potatoes are tender and the sauce has thickened. (Use a fork to stir gently to avoid breaking up the potatoes.)

3. Taste and adjust the seasoning, adding salt and pepper, if needed. Transfer the mixture to warm bowls and serve immediately.

PORK BRAISED WITH CELERIAC & ORANGE

In many parts of China, slow-cooked casseroles are popular during the cold winter months. Orange, star anise, and chili bean sauce are particularly good with pork and celeriac.

SERVES: 4

PREP TIME: 20 MINS PLUS MARINATING

COOK TIME: 2¼ HRS

INGREDIENTS

2 pounds pork shoulder, cubed

3 tablespoons olive oil

1 head of celeriac, cut into 2-inch sticks

2 small leeks, cut into 2-inch strips

3 carrots, cut into 2-inch strips

1 cup chicken stock

cooked rice, to serve

MARINADE

thinly pared rind and juice of 1 orange

1–2 whole star anise

2 tablespoons dark soy sauce

1 tablespoon honey

1-inch piece fresh ginger, grated

3 garlic cloves, finely chopped

2 teaspoons Chinese chili bean sauce

1. Place the pork in a large bowl. Add all the marinade ingredients, stir well, cover, and chill in the refrigerator for 3 hours or overnight.

2. Preheat the oven to 250°F. Remove the pork from the marinade using a slotted spoon and transfer to a plate, discarding the orange peel and star anise. Reserve the marinade.

3. Heat 1 tablespoon of the oil in a large skillet and add half the pork pieces. Cook for 2 minutes, then turn the pieces over and cook for an additional 2 minutes.

4. Transfer the pork and the cooking juices to a casserole dish. Repeat with 1 tablespoon of the oil and the remaining pork and transfer to the casserole dish.

5. Add the remaining oil to the skillet, then add the celeriac, leeks, and carrots and cook, stirring occasionally, until the leeks are soft.

6. Transfer the vegetables to the casserole dish, strain the marinade over the vegetables, and add

the stock. Cover and cook in the preheated oven for 1 hour.

7. Stir the pork and vegetables, cover, and return to the oven for an additional 1 hour. Serve with cooked rice.

WHAT'S COOKING?

Cooking root vegetables in different ways produces different tastes and textures. Regardless of how you decide to cook them, use roots of a similar size, or cut them into even pieces so that they cook at the same rate. Put peeled potato, celeriac, and parsnip straight into water to stop them from browning.

STEAMING

This is a healthy alternative to boiling, and a handy technique to partly soften root vegetables before roasting or grilling. Because they aren't in direct contact with liquid, they don't become waterlogged and fewer nutrients leach into the water. If you have never tried steaming, it's worth investing in a universal steamer insert.

BOILING

Boiling is the simplest method for the majority of roots, but remember that the turbulent action of fast-boiling liquid can break up the starchier ones—Jerusalem artichokes, yams, and mealy potatoes, for example. It's best to start them in cold water and turn down the heat once boiling, so they cook at a gentler pace.

STOVE-TOP GRILLING

This works well for denser roots, such as rutabaga or celeriac. Lightly steam them, then cut into thick slices and brush with oil. You will need a heavy, cast iron pan, preferably with ridges for producing appealing brown stripes. The direct heat quickly seals in the juices and crisps the outside.

SAUTÉING

Sautéing brings anemic-looking roots to life. They develop intense flavors, a crisp texture, and become sweetly caramelized. Slice them first and sauté in a roomy pan. If you overcrowd them, they will steam instead of becoming brown and crisp.

ROASTING

The dry heat of the oven caramelizes natural sugars in root vegetables, making them brown and sticky in the process. Give them plenty of space and use a shallow roasting pan instead a deep one with high sides, so that heat can circulate unimpeded.

CREAMED CHICKEN WITH JERUSALEM ARTICHOKES

SERVES: 2   **PREP TIME: 15 MINS**   **COOK TIME: 25 MINS**

INGREDIENTS

2 tablespoons butter

1 onion, finely chopped

1⅓ cups sliced Jerusalem artichokes

1 cup water

½ cup white wine

2 fresh tarragon sprigs or ½ teaspoon dried tarragon

2 (4-ounce) skinless, boneless chicken breasts

1 teaspoon Dijon mustard

3 tablespoons crème fraîche

salt and pepper, to taste

chopped fresh tarragon, to garnish (optional)

cooked rice, to serve

1. Melt the butter in a large skillet over medium heat, add the onions, and cook for 4–5 minutes, or until soft. Add the artichokes, water, wine, and tarragon. Bring to a boil, then reduce the heat and simmer, covered, for 5 minutes, or until the artichokes are just tender.

2. Cut each chicken breast into four pieces and add to the skillet. Season with salt and pepper and continue to cook, stirring, for 10 minutes, or until the chicken is cooked through and shows no traces of pink.

3. Remove the tarragon sprigs and stir in the mustard and crème fraîche. Increase the heat and let the sauce simmer and thicken. Divide between two warm plates and garnish with chopped tarragon, if using. Serve immediately with cooked rice.

SWEET POTATO CURRY WITH LENTILS

This sweet potato curry is nutritious and filling, so it is ideal for spice lovers with big appetites! Sweet potato is high in carotenes, lowers cholesterol, and is a good food to help dieters ward off hunger.

SERVES: 4　　　　**PREP TIME: 15 MINS**　　　　**COOK TIME: 45 MINS**

INGREDIENTS

1 teaspoon vegetable oil

1 small sweet potato, cut into bite-size cubes

1 small Yukon gold, white round, or red-skinned potato, cut into bite-size cubes

1 small onion, finely chopped

1 small garlic clove, finely chopped

1 small fresh green chile, seeded and chopped

½ teaspoon ground ginger

¼ cup green lentils

⅓–½ cup hot vegetable stock

½ teaspoon garam masala

1 tablespoon plain yogurt

pepper, to taste

1. Heat the oil in a saucepan with a lid and sauté the sweet potato over medium heat, turning occasionally, for 5 minutes.

2. Meanwhile, cook the potato in a saucepan of boiling water for 6 minutes, until almost cooked. Drain and set aside.

3. Remove the sweet potato from the pan with a slotted spoon, then add the onion to the pan. Cook, stirring occasionally, for 5 minutes, or until transparent. Add the garlic, chile, and ginger and stir for 1 minute.

4. Return the sweet potato to the pan with the boiled potato and the lentils, half the stock, and the garam masala and season with pepper. Stir well to combine, bring to a simmer, and cover.

5. Reduce the heat and simmer for 20 minutes, adding the rest of the stock if the curry looks too dry. Stir in the yogurt and serve immediately.

ON THE SIDE

Roasted Root Vegetables 100

Mashed Potatoes with Leek & Cabbage 102

Crispy Potato Slices 104

Mashed Potatoes with Rutabaga 106

Sugar-Glazed Parsnips 108

Caramelized Sweet Potatoes 110

Keep It Fresh 112

Root Vegetable Fries 114

Roasted Potato Wedges with Shallots 116

Mashed Sweet Potato with Parsley Butter 118

Vichy Carrots with Parsley 120

Dressed Beet Salad 122

Roasted Carrot Dip with Feta 124

Beet & Chickpea Hummus 126

ROASTED ROOT VEGETABLES

SERVES: 4-6 **PREP TIME: 15 MINS** **COOK TIME: 1 HR**

INGREDIENTS

3 parsnips, cut into 2-inch chunks

4 baby turnips, cut into quarters

3 carrots, cut into 2-inch chunks

½ butternut squash, cut into 2-inch chunks

3 sweet potatoes, cut into 2-inch chunks

2 garlic cloves, finely chopped

2 tablespoons chopped fresh rosemary

2 tablespoons chopped fresh thyme

2 teaspoon chopped fresh sage

3 tablespoons olive oil

salt and pepper, to taste

2 tablespoons chopped fresh mixed herbs, such as parsley, thyme, and mint, to garnish

1. Preheat the oven to 425°F.

2. Arrange all the vegetables in a single layer in a large roasting pan. Sprinkle with the garlic, rosemary, thyme, and sage. Pour the oil over the vegetables and season well with salt and pepper.

3. Toss together all the ingredients until they are well mixed and coated with the oil (you can marinate at this stage to let the flavors be absorbed).

4. Roast the vegetables at the top of the preheated oven for 50–60 minutes, until they are cooked and nicely browned. Turn the vegetables over halfway through the cooking time. Serve immediately, garnished with the mixed herbs.

HERO TIPS

These delicious roasted root vegetables are crisp and golden on the outside and soft and fluffy on the inside! They make a great accompaniment to a traditional roast dinner or to any baked dish, such as a lasagna or a tuna casserole.

MASHED POTATOES WITH LEEK & CABBAGE

This dish of fluffy potatoes with leeks and cabbage is a classic Irish dish, known as Colcannon, that is often served on St. Patrick's Day. It even has a traditional Irish folk song written about it, of the same name.

SERVES: 4   **PREP TIME: 15 MINS**   **COOK TIME: 20-25 MINS**

INGREDIENTS

2½ cups shredded green cabbage

2 Yukon gold or russet potatoes, diced

1 large leek, chopped

3 tablespoons milk

pinch of freshly grated nutmeg

pat of butter

salt and pepper, to taste

1. Cook the shredded cabbage in a saucepan of boiling salted water for 7–10 minutes. Drain thoroughly and set aside.

2. Meanwhile, bring a separate saucepan of salted water to a boil and add the potatoes and leek. Reduce the heat and simmer for 15–20 minutes, or until they are cooked through. Drain and then stir in the milk and the freshly grated nutmeg. Thoroughly mash together the potatoes and leek.

3. Add the drained cabbage to the mashed potato-and-leek mixture, season, and mix together well.

4. Spoon the mixture into a warm serving dish, making a hollow in the center with the back of a spoon. Place the butter in the hollow and serve the colcannon immediately, while it is still hot.

CRISPY POTATO SLICES

SERVES: 4   **PREP TIME: 10 MINS**   **COOK TIME: 25 MINS**

INGREDIENTS

4 russet, white round, or red-skinned potatoes

¼ cup goose or duck fat, or 3 tablespoons butter with 1 tablespoon olive oil

salt, to taste

1. Bring a large saucepan of lightly salted water to a boil. Add the potatoes, bring back to a boil, and cook for 5 minutes. Drain the potatoes and, when they are cool enough to handle, peel and cut into thin slices or small cubes.

2. Melt the fat or butter and oil in a large, heavy sauté pan or skillet over high heat, until hot but not smoking. Pour off any excess fat so you are left with ¼ inch of fat.

3. Add the potatoes to the pan, spread out so they are evenly distributed, and reduce the heat to medium. Sauté the potatoes, shaking the pan and turning them occasionally, for 10–12 minutes, or until they are golden brown and crisp on the outside. Use a slotted spoon to transfer the potatoes to a plate lined with paper towels and drain well. Season with salt and serve immediately.

MASHED POTATOES WITH RUTABAGA

This Scottish dish, known as Neeps and Tatties, is a mix of mashed rutabaga (neeps) and potatoes (tatties), traditionally served on Burns Night with haggis. This dish also makes a good accompaniment to roast meats, stews, or casseroles.

SERVES: 5   **PREP TIME: 15 MINS**   **COOK TIME: 20-25 MINS**

INGREDIENTS

1 rutabaga, diced

2 Yukon gold or russet potatoes, diced

4 tablespoons butter, plus extra to serve

whole nutmeg, for grating, to taste

salt and pepper, to taste

fresh parsley sprigs, to garnish

1. Bring a large saucepan of lightly salted water to a boil. Add the rutabaga and potatoes and cook for 20 minutes, until soft. Test with the point of a knife—if not cooked, return to the heat for an additional 5 minutes. Drain well.

2. Return the rutabaga and potatoes to the empty saucepan and heat for a few moments to make sure they are dry. Add the butter and mash with a potato masher until smooth.

3. Season well with salt and pepper and stir through. Grate nutmeg into the mash and serve immediately, garnished with the parsley and with a pat of butter on top.

HERO TIPS

The rutabaga is a cross between a cabbage and a turnip. Another way to serve this dish is to add chives and onions to the recipe—this version of the dish is known in Scotland as clapshot.

107

SUGAR-GLAZED PARSNIPS

These gently caramelized parsnips are a great dish to serve with roasted meats or a nut roast. They are also perfect for special occasions, such as Christmas or Easter dinners.

SERVES: 8   **PREP TIME: 5 MINS**   **COOK TIME: 40 MINS**

INGREDIENTS

24 small parsnips, sliced lengthwise

about 1 teaspoon salt

1 stick butter

1 cup firmly packed light brown sugar

1. Place the parsnips in a saucepan, add just enough water to cover, then add the salt. Bring to a boil, reduce the heat, cover, and simmer for 20–25 minutes, until tender. Drain well.

2. Melt the butter in a heavy saucepan or wok. Add the parsnips and toss well. Sprinkle with the sugar, then cook, stirring continuously to prevent the sugar from sticking to the pan or burning.

3. Cook the parsnips for 10–15 minutes, until golden and glazed. Transfer to a warm serving dish and serve immediately.

HERO TIPS

The parsnip is a close relative of the carrot and is similarly good for your health. It contains a lot of dietary fiber to aid the digestive system.

CARAMELIZED SWEET POTATOES

SERVES: 4   **PREP TIME: 10 MINS**   **COOK TIME: 1¼ HRS**

INGREDIENTS

3 sweet potatoes, washed but not peeled

4 tablespoons butter, plus extra for greasing

¼ cup firmly packed brown sugar, maple syrup, or honey

2 tablespoons orange or pineapple juice

⅓ cup pineapple chunks (optional)

pinch of ground cinnamon, nutmeg, or allspice (optional)

salt

1. Bring a large saucepan of lightly salted water to a boil. Add the sweet potatoes, bring back to a boil, and cook for about 30–45 minutes, until just tender. Remove from the heat and drain well. Let cool slightly, then peel.

2. Preheat the oven to 400°F. Grease an ovenproof dish. Thickly slice the sweet potatoes and arrange in a single overlapping layer in the prepared dish.

3. Cut the butter into small cubes and dot over the top.

4. Sprinkle with the sugar and orange juice. Add the pineapple chunks and spices, if using. Bake in the preheated oven for 30–40 minutes, basting occasionally, until golden brown.

5. Remove from the oven and serve hot, straight from the dish.

HERO TIPS

Sweet potatoes are low in calories and low on the glycemic index, making them an ideal root vegetable for dieters.

KEEP IT FRESH!

Root vegetables stay freshest in a cool, dark, dry, well-ventilated place, not necessarily in the refrigerator (see below). Freshly harvested, they can be stored for months in a basement or frost-free garage. Depending on when they are harvested, store-bought roots can be kept for several days in a cool room. Failing this, store them in a ventilated drawer (wicker or perforated metal), away from heat-producing appliances, such as the stove or refrigerator, and preferably protected in a light-excluding drawstring cotton bag to prevent sprouting. There are several on the market specifically for storing root vegetables.

Roots that can survive the chill of the refrigerator should be stored, unwashed, in the crisp drawer, where the temperature is less

arctic. They are best wrapped in newspaper or a paper bag. Paper absorbs moisture, providing the slightly humid but well-ventilated atmosphere that most roots need. In some cases, a sealed plastic bag is preferable; radishes, for example, need an enclosed moist environment.

If you buy roots with leaves and stems, remove these before storing, leaving a short length of stem attached to avoid exposing the flesh. Leaves may give the impression of freshness, but they rot quickly and the root itself loses moisture through them.

STORAGE TIMES

The following times are a guide for storing store-bought vegetables in the refrigerator, a cool, dry place, or ventilated drawer. The time will depend on when they were harvested, where and how they have been stored after harvesting, and how long they have been on sale.

Beets: Seven to ten days.

Carrots: Young, three to four days; mature, one to two weeks.

Celeriacs: One week, wrapped in plastic wrap to prevent drying.

Jerusalem artichokes: Seven to ten days.

Parsnips: One week.

Potatoes: One week, ideally in a light-proof cloth bag; do not store in the refrigerator, or they will become unpleasantly sweet.

Radishes: Three to four days in the refrigerator, wrapped in damp paper towels in a sealed plastic bag.

Rutabagas: Three to four weeks.

Sweet potatoes: Three to four weeks.

Turnips: Young, one week; mature, two to three weeks.

Yams: Seven to ten days; do not store in the refrigerator because this causes rotting.

ROOT VEGETABLE FRIES

These root vegetable fries make a great alternative to traditional potato skinny fries or wedges. They use less oil than traditional fries as well and so are better for you, too.

SERVES: 4   **PREP TIME: 10 MINS**   **COOK TIME: 25 MINS**

INGREDIENTS

2 pounds of any combination of parsnips, rutabagas, turnips, and carrots, cut into ¼-inch strips

2 tablespoons vegetable oil

1 teaspoon salt

sea salt, to taste

1. Preheat the oven to 450°F.

2. Toss the cut vegetables with the oil and salt. Spread the vegetables in a single layer on a large baking sheet and bake in the preheated oven for about 20 minutes, flipping them halfway through cooking, until they are golden brown and cooked through. Remove from the oven and preheat the broiler to medium.

3. Put under the preheated broiler for 2–3 minutes, until they begin to become crisp. Flip them over and return to the broiler for an additional 2 minutes to crisp the other side. Serve immediately, sprinkled with sea salt.

ROASTED POTATO WEDGES WITH SHALLOTS

SERVES: 4   **PREP TIME: 10 MINS**   **COOK TIME: 1 HR**

INGREDIENTS

2¼ pounds new potatoes or russets

⅓ cup olive oil

2 fresh rosemary sprigs

6 ounces baby shallots

2 garlic cloves, sliced

salt and pepper, to taste

1. Preheat the oven to 400°F. If using larger potatoes, peel them. Cut the potatoes into thick wedges. Put the potatoes in a large saucepan of lightly salted water and bring to a boil. Reduce the heat and simmer for 5 minutes.

2. Heat the oil in a large roasting pan on the stove. Drain the potatoes well and add to the roasting pan. Strip the leaves from the rosemary sprigs, chop finely, and sprinkle over the potatoes.

3. Roast the potatoes in the preheated oven for 35 minutes, turning twice during cooking. Add the shallots and garlic and roast for an additional 15 minutes, until golden brown. Season with salt and pepper.

4. Transfer to a warm serving dish and serve immediately.

HERO TIPS

It is best to use a small, waxy potato for this recipe, such as new potatoes or a small variety. Potatoes are rich in minerals that help the functioning of your brain and muscles to keep you thinking and moving youthfully.

MASHED SWEET POTATO WITH PARSLEY BUTTER

SERVES: 4   **PREP TIME: 10 MINS**   **COOK TIME: 25 MINS**

INGREDIENTS

5 tablespoons butter, softened

2 tablespoons chopped fresh parsley

6 sweet potatoes, scrubbed

salt

1. Reserving 2 tablespoons, put the butter into a bowl with the parsley and beat together. Turn out onto a piece of aluminum foil or plastic wrap, shape into a block, and chill in the refrigerator until required.

2. Cut the sweet potatoes into even chunks. Bring a large saucepan of lightly salted water to a boil, add the sweet potatoes, bring back to a boil, and cook, covered, for 15–20 minutes, until tender.

3. Drain the potatoes well, then cover the pan with a clean dish towel and let stand for 2 minutes. Remove the skins and mash with a potato masher until fluffy.

4. Add the reserved butter to the sweet potatoes and stir in evenly. Spoon into a serving dish and serve hot, topped with pats of parsley butter.

VICHY CARROTS WITH PARSLEY

This dish originates from France and is named after the town of Vichy in the center of France. To be authentic, the recipe must be made with Vichy mineral water but any other type will be fine, too.

SERVES: 4-6   **PREP TIME: 10-15 MINS**   **COOK TIME: 10-15 MINS**

INGREDIENTS

2 tablespoons unsalted butter
8 carrots, cut into ¼-inch slices
1 tablespoon sugar
bottle of Vichy mineral water
salt and pepper, to taste
2 tablespoons chopped fresh flat-leaf parsley

1. Melt the butter in a large, heavy saucepan over medium–high heat. Stir in the carrots, then stir in the sugar and season with salt and pepper.

2. Pour over enough Vichy water to cover the carrots by 2 inches and bring to a boil. Reduce the heat to medium and let the carrots simmer, uncovered, stirring occasionally, until they are tender, all the liquid has been absorbed, and they are coated in a thin glaze.

3. Adjust the seasoning, if necessary, transfer to a serving dish, and stir in the parsley. Serve immediately.

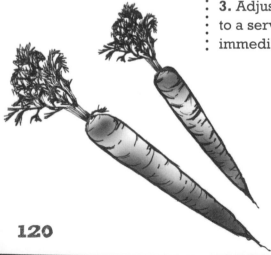

120

DRESSED BEET SALAD

PREP TIME: 20 MINS
PLUS CHILLING

COOK TIME: 25-40 MINS

INGREDIENTS

11 raw beets (about 2 pounds)
¼ cup extra virgin olive oil
1½ tablespoons
red wine vinegar
2 garlic cloves, finely chopped
2 scallions, minced
salt, to taste

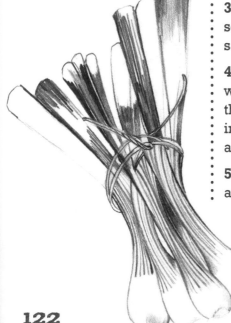

1. Carefully remove the roots from the beets without cutting into the skin, then cut off all but 1 inch of the stems. Gently rub the beets under cold running water, without splitting the skins, to remove any dirt.

2. Put the beets in a saucepan with water enough to cover and bring to a boil. Cover, reduce the heat slightly, and cook for 25–40 minutes, depending on the size, until the largest beet is tender when pierced with the tip of a sharp knife.

3. Meanwhile, put the oil, vinegar, garlic, and scallions into a jar with a screw-top lid, season with salt, and shake until emulsified, then set aside.

4. Drain the beets and rinse under cold running water until cool enough to handle, then peel away the skins. Thickly chop or slice the beets, then put in a bowl and pour the dressing over them. Cover and chill in the refrigerator for at least 1 hour.

5. To serve, gently toss the salad and transfer to a serving bowl.

ROASTED CARROT DIP WITH FETA

The bright orange color of carrots indicates they have high levels of beta carotene and alpha carotene. These give them the ability to rejuvenate your skin and other organs.

SERVES: 4-6   **PREP TIME: 15 MINS**   **COOK TIME: 40 MINS**

INGREDIENTS

8 carrots (about 1 pound), thickly sliced

½ cup extra virgin olive oil

2 teaspoons cumin seeds, toasted and ground

⅔ cup crumbled feta cheese or fresh firm goat cheese

salt and pepper, to taste

1 small bunch of fresh cilantro, finely chopped, to garnish

1. Preheat the oven to 400°F. Put the carrots in an ovenproof dish, pour the oil over them, and cover the dish with aluminum foil. Bake in the preheated oven for about 25 minutes.

2. Meanwhile, heat a dry, heavy skillet over medium–high heat. Add the cumin seeds and cook for 3–4 minutes, tossing the seeds frequently, until lightly toasted and fragrant. Let cool, then grind, using a mortar and pestle or an electric grinder, to form a coarse powder.

3. Remove the foil from the ovenproof dish, toss in the ground cumin seeds, and bake for an additional 15 minutes, or until tender.

4. Mash the carrots with a fork, combining them with the oil in the dish, or blend them to a paste in a blender or food processor. Season with salt and pepper and spoon into a serving dish. Sprinkle the crumbled feta cheese over the top and garnish with the cilantro. Serve warm or at room temperature.

BEET & CHICKPEA HUMMUS

This is a great twist on the traditional hummus, with the vibrant red and tangy flavor of the beet really adding visual impact and a fuller flavor.

SERVES: 4-6   **PREP TIME: 10 MINS**   **COOK TIME: NONE**

INGREDIENTS

1 (15-ounce) can chickpeas, drained and rinsed
1 garlic clove, coarsely chopped
2 cooked beets
1½ tablespoons tahini
juice of ½ lemon
3 tablespoons olive oil
salt and pepper, to taste
vegetable sticks, to serve

1. Place the chickpeas, garlic, and beets in a food processor or blender and process until broken up into the size of crumbs.

2. Add the tahini and lemon juice and process again, pouring in the olive oil until the hummus is the consistency you prefer. Season with salt and pepper.

3. Serve the hummus with vegetable sticks.

HERO TIPS

The dark green, purple-tinged leaves of the beet are an edible vegetable, too, and can be sliced or steamed. Like the root, they are rich in vitamins, minerals, and carotenes.

INDEX

apples: Sweet Potato & Apple Soup 16

bacon
    Slow-Cooked Potato Stew 88
    Yam, Rutabaga & Mushroom Hash 48
beef
    Yam & Beef Stew with Couscous 32
    Yam-Topped Beef Casserole 38
beets 6, 9, 30, 42, 74–75, 113
    Beet & Chickpea Hummus 126
    Beet Borscht Soup 22
    Beet Burgers in a Bun 34
    Beet, Lobster & Spinach
        Risotto 84
    Dressed Beet Salad 122
    Raw Beet & Pecan Salad 56
    Roasted Beet Packages 72
bell peppers: Stir-Fried Chicken &
    Rutabaga 66
broccoli: Baked Potato, Broccoli &
    Peanut 62
butternut squash: Roasted Root
    Vegetables 100

cabbage: Mashed Potatoes with Leek
    & Cabbage 102
carrots 6, 9, 30, 75, 113
    Baked Root Vegetable & Rosemary
        Cake 86
    Beet Burgers in a Bun 34
    Carrot Sausages & Mashed
        Potatoes 26
    Carrot & Orange Stir-Fry 44
    Carrot Upside-Down Tart 80
    Lamb & Turnip Stew 54
    Pork Braised with Celeriac &
        Orange 90
    Roasted Carrot Dip with Feta 124
    Roasted Root Soup with Ginger 20
    Roasted Root Vegetables 100
    Root Vegetable Fries 114
    Vichy Carrots with Parsley 120
    Yam-Topped Beef Casserole 38
cauliflower: Potato & Radish Salad 60
celeriac 6, 30, 43, 113
    Baked Root Vegetable & Rosemary
        Cake 86
    Celeriac Salad with Crab 52
    Celeriac Soup with Cheese Pastry
        Sticks 14
    Pork Braised with Celeriac &
        Orange 90
cheese
    Beet, Lobster & Spinach
        Risotto 84
    Celeriac Soup with Cheese Pastry
        Sticks 14
    New Potato, Feta & Herb Frittata 46
    Parsnip Layered Casserole 58
    Roasted Carrot Dip with Feta 124
chicken
    Creamed Chicken with Jerusalem
        Artichokes 94
    Stir-Fried Chicken & Rutabaga 66
chickpeas
    Beet & Chickpea Hummus 126
    Yam & Beef Stew with Couscous 32
corn kernels: Potato & Corn Fritters
    with Relish 24

eggs
    New Potato, Feta & Herb Frittata 46
    Yam, Rutabaga & Mushroom Hash 48

fish & seafood
    Beet, Lobster & Spinach
        Risotto 84

Celeriac Salad with Crab 52
Pan-Cooked Tuna with Radish
    Relish 64

green beans: Potato & Radish
    Salad 60

ham: Caramelized Rutabaga & Ham
    Pie 76

Jerusalem artichokes 6, 30, 113
    Creamed Chicken with Jerusalem
        Artichokes 94
    Jerusalem Artichoke & Hazelnut
        Gratin 50
    Jerusalem Artichoke Soup 18
    Jerusalem Artichokes with Tomato
        Sauce 36

lamb: Lamb & Turnip Stew 54
leeks
    Carrot & Orange Stir-Fry 44
    Mashed Potatoes with Leek &
        Cabbage 102
    Pork Braised with Celeriac &
        Orange 90
    Sweet Potato & Apple Soup 16
    Yam-Topped Beef Casserole 38
lentils: Sweet Potato Curry with
    Lentils 96

mushrooms: Yam, Rutabaga &
    Mushroom Hash 48

nuts
    Baked Potatoes, Broccoli &
        Peanuts 62
    Beet Burgers in a Bun 34
    Carrot Sausages & Mashed
        Potatoes 26
    Carrot & Orange Stir-Fry 44
    Jerusalem Artichoke & Hazelnut
        Gratin 50
    Potato Gnocchi with Walnut
        Pesto 78
    Raw Beet & Pecan Salad 56

parsnips 7, 30, 113
    Baked Root Vegetable & Rosemary
        Cake 86
    Parsnip Layered Casserole 58
    Roasted Root Vegetables 100
    Root Vegetable Fries 114
    Spiced Parsnip Gratin with Ginger
        Cream 82
    Sugar-Glazed Parsnips 108
pastry
    Caramelized Rutabaga &
        Ham Pie 76
    Carrot Upside-Down Tart 80
    Celeriac Soup with Cheese Pastry
        Sticks 14
peas: Lamb & Turnip Stew 54
Pork Braised with Celeriac &
    Orange 90
potatoes 7, 31, 113
    Baked Potatoes, Broccoli &
        Peanuts 62
    Carrot Sausages & Mashed
        Potatoes 26
    Crispy Potato Slices 104
    Lamb & Turnip Stew 54
    Mashed Potatoes with Leek &
        Cabbage 102
    Mashed Potatoes with
        Rutabaga 106

New Potato, Feta & Herb Frittata 46
Potato & Corn Fritters with
    Relish 24
Potato & Radish Salad 60
Potato Gnocchi with Walnut
    Pesto 78
Roasted Potato Wedges with
    Shallots 116
Slow-Cooked Potato Stew 88
Yam & Beef Stew with Couscous 32

radishes 7, 31, 113
    Pan-Cooked Tuna with Radish
        Relish 64
    Potato & Radish Salad 60
    Raw Beet & Pecan Salad 56
root vegetables
    boiling 92
    buying 12–13, 30–31
    grilling, stove-top 93
    growing 74–75
    health benefits 8–9
    organic 13
    preparing 42–43
    roasting 93
    sautéing 93
    steaming 92
    storage 112–113
rutabaga 7, 31, 113
    Mashed Potatoes with Rutabaga 106
    Caramelized Rutabaga &
        Ham Pie 76
    Roasted Root Soup with Ginger 20
    Root Vegetable Fries 114
    Stir-Fried Chicken & Rutabaga 66
    Yam, Rutabaga & Mushroom Hash 48
    Yam-Topped Beef Casserole 38

spinach
    Beet, Lobster & Spinach Risotto 84
    New Potato, Feta & Herb Frittata 46
    Potato & Radish Salad 60
    Sweet Potato Pancakes 28
sweet potatoes 7, 31, 113
    Caramelized Sweet Potatoes 110
    Mashed Sweet Potato with Parsley
        Butter 118
    Roasted Root Soup with Ginger 20
    Roasted Root Vegetables 100
    Sweet Potato & Apple Soup 16
    Sweet Potato Curry with Lentils 96
    Sweet Potato Pancakes 28
    Sweet Potato Ravioli with Sage
        Butter 70

tomatoes
    Beet Borscht Soup 22
    Jerusalem Artichokes with Tomato
        Sauce 36
    Parsnip Layered Casserole 58
    Potato & Corn Fritters with Relish 24
    Slow-Cooked Potato Stew 88
    Yam & Beef Stew with Couscous 32
    Yam-Topped Beef Casserole 38
turnips 7, 31, 113
    Lamb & Turnip Stew 54
    Roasted Root Vegetables 100
    Root Vegetable Fries 114

yams 7, 31, 113
    Yam & Beef Stew with Couscous 32
    Yam, Rutabaga & Mushroom Hash 48
    Yam-Topped Beef Casserole 38

zucchini: Beet Burgers in a Bun 34